**Huntingdon Area
Middle School Library**
Huntingdon, Pa.

Class No. *Acc. No.*

587.8
PEA

AMAZING SCIENCE

TYRANNOSAURUS REX

AND OTHER

DINOSAUR WONDERS

Q.L. PEARCE

Illustrated by Mary Ann Fraser

Julian Messner

To Jennifer, Jamie, and Chardonnay —Q.L. Pearce
To Ian —Mary Ann Fraser

Acknowledgments

With thanks to Peggy Kayser of the Skirball Museum, Los Angeles, for her critical review of the manuscript.

Library of Congress Cataloging-in-Publication Data
Pearce, Q. L. (Querida Lee)
  Tyrannosaurus Rex and other dinosaur wonders / Q.L. Pearce ; illustrated by Mary Ann Fraser.
    p. cm.
  Includes bibliographical references (p.   ).
  Summary: Examines the different kinds of dinosaurs that dominated the Earth during the Age of Reptiles.
  1. Dinosaurs—Juvenile literature. [1. Dinosaurs.] I. Fraser, Mary Ann, ill. II. Title. III. Series.
QE862.D5P43 1990   80-6014
587.8'1—dc20   CIP

ISBN 0-671-70687-X (lib. bdg.)
ISBN 0-671-70688-8 (pbk.)

Text copyright © 1990 by RGA Publishing Group, Inc.
Illustrations copyright © 1990 by RGA Publishing Group, Inc.
All rights reserved including the right of
reproduction in whole or in part in any form.
Published by Julian Messner, a division of
Silver Burdett Press, Inc., Simon & Schuster, Inc.
Prentice Hall Bldg., Englewood Cliffs, NJ 07632.

JULIAN MESSNER and colophon are trademarks of
Simon & Schuster, Inc.
Manufactured in the United States of America.

Lib. ed.:   10 9 8 7 6 5 4 3 2 1
Paper ed.:   10 9 8 7 6 5 4 3 2 1

Contents

The Ancient Rulers	5
The Dinosaur World	7
A Reptilian Beginning	9
The Smallest Dinosaurs	11
Ancient Sea Serpents	13
Reptiles in the Air	15
The Giants	17
Plates and Spikes	19
The Boneheads	21
The Armored Tanks	23
Horns and Frills	25
The Tyrant King	27
The Duckbills	29
Dangerous Deinonychus	31
Speed Demons	33
The Fishing Dinosaur	35
Sail-Backed Dinosaurs	37
The Colorful Dinosaurs	39
South America: The Island	41
Warm Blood or Cold Blood?	43
Archaeopteryx: Bird or Dinosaur?	45
The Dinosaur Egg	47
Dinosaur Nurseries	49
An Enemy from Space?	51
The Survivors	53
The First Mammals	55
The Bone Wars	57
The Mummies	59
Dinosaur Trackers	61
Lessons from the Past	62
For Further Reading	63
Index	64

The Ancient Rulers

We shall probably never know when the first dinosaur bones were uncovered by curious humans. More than 1,700 years ago, Chinese scholars noted the discovery of huge animal bones, which they decided were the remains of ancient sacred dragons. In the late 1600s, a drawing of an unusually large bone appeared in the book *The Natural History of Oxfordshire* by Robert Plot. Plot mistakenly identified the bone as belonging to a giant elephant. Nearly 200 years later, new discoveries led scientists to realize that these bones did not belong to any known creatures. They were the remains of strange reptiles that had been both magnificent and frightening. In 1841, Richard Owen named these ancient beasts by combining the Greek word *deinos*, meaning "terrible," with *sauros*, meaning "lizard." From that time forward, the creatures were known as the dinosaurs. No human has ever seen or heard a living dinosaur, yet no animal has so gripped the human imagination.

The first dinosaurs appeared on Earth some 225 MYA (million years ago) and mysteriously died out about 65 MYA. Thus, the dinosaurs ruled our planet for approximately 160 million years. That is an amazingly long time, considering that humans have lived on Earth for only about a million and a half years! To imagine what a long stay the dinosaurs had on Earth, let's pretend for a moment that time has sped up, and for every second that ticks by on the clock, one year speeds by. In that case, the dinosaurs would have appeared nearly seven years ago and disappeared about two years ago. The first primitive humans would have turned up just a few weeks ago. Your parents would probably be less than one minute old!

The Dinosaur World

The dinosaurs lived during the Mesozoic (or "middle life") Era. Scientists divide this huge span of time into three sections. The first part, called the Triassic Period, lasted roughly from 250 to 215 MYA. The Triassic Period was named for three rock layers that formed at that time. Earth was quite a different place then. The warm, dry climate changed little with the seasons. The land, much of it desert dotted with volcanoes, was a single continent called Pangaea (pan-JEE-uh), or "all Earth." Ferns and cycads (SY-kudz), plants similar to palm trees, grew along the shores of shallow lakes. This was the land of the first small dinosaurs.

The Jurassic Period (215 to 145 MYA) was named for the Jura Mountains in the Alps, where rock layers from the period can be found. During this time, huge Pangaea split into two smaller continents, Laurasia and Gondwanaland (gahn-DWAH-nuh-land). The weather was more changeable than it had been earlier. Dry spells followed periods of rain and flooding. The land became lush with tree ferns and tall conifers (cone-bearing trees). It was a time of giants. Huge *Apatosaurus* browsed among the trees, while meat-eaters such as *Allosaurus* stalked their prey.

The Cretaceous (krih-TAY-shus) Period (145 to 65 MYA) was named for layers of chalk that formed at that time. During this time of great change, the continents splintered apart. A huge inland sea connected the Gulf of Mexico to the Arctic Ocean! Oaks and magnolias replaced ferns and conifers. Great herds of horned, beaked, and armored dinosaurs shared the land with the fiercest flesh-eater of all time, *Tyrannosaurus rex*.

The Mesozoic Era time chart outlines the lifespan of the ancient dinosaurs.

A Reptilian Beginning

The first reptiles (not yet true dinosaurs) were small, lizardlike creatures that lived in pre-Triassic times. They had legs that extended sideways from the body and then bent down at the knee, so that their stomachs rested on the ground. Because of this sprawling posture, their legs couldn't bear much weight and these reptiles couldn't move very fast.

Shortly before the Mesozoic Era began, during a time known as the Permian Period, a new class of reptiles, called the thecodonts, developed. The thecodonts differed from most reptiles of that time in several ways. First, thecodont teeth grew from small sockets in the jaw, rather than from the surface of the jawbone. In fact, *thecodont* means "socket toothed." There was another difference, too: Some thecodonts, such as the tiny, two-foot-long *Euparkeria* (yoo-par-KAIR-ee-uh), developed slightly longer hind legs that were positioned further underneath the body. This more efficient arrangement gave *Euparkeria* the ability to outrun both its predators and its competitors for food.

The first true dinosaurs differed from the thecodonts in leg structure. They appeared late in the Triassic Period and improved on what the thecodonts had begun. *Coelophysis* (seel-o-FY-sis), or "hollow form," for example, stood with its long hind legs held directly beneath its slender body. This made the creature faster and more agile than other reptiles, an advantage when competing for food. With its snakelike tail held up for balance, this 10-foot-long dinosaur raced in small packs across the dry sands, searching for prey. It probably ate any small animal it could catch. There is evidence that this primitive dinosaur even ate its own young.

With its longer hind legs, tiny Euparkeria *could outrun both its predators and its competitors for food.*

Tyrannosaurus rex

Saltopus

The Smallest Dinosaurs

Dinosaurs are divided into two main groups according to the shape of their hip bones. Bird-hipped dinosaurs, called ornithicians (or-nih-THIH-shee-unz), were plant-eaters. Lizard-hipped dinosaurs, the sauricians (sore-IH-shee-unz), included both plant- and meat-eaters. The sauricians were the first dinosaurs to develop. Although this group would someday include the largest land animals that had ever lived, the *first* sauricians were among the smallest dinosaurs.

Saltopus, which lived during the Triassic Period, was no taller than a house cat and measured only two feet long from nose to tail. It was probably a fast runner, kicking up clouds of dust as it shot after tasty insects or small, speedy lizards. At one time, people thought that this little animal may have hopped or jumped from place to place. That may be why it was named *Saltopus,* or "leaping foot."

Compsognathus (kahmp-so-NAY-thus), or "pretty jaw," was a chicken-sized dinosaur that lived well into the Jurassic Period. Although it measured about two feet long, most of that was neck and tail. *Compsognathus* weighed barely eight pounds. It is certain that lizards were a part of this dinosaur's diet because scientists discovered the remains of a *Compsognathus* with dainty lizard bones inside it.

Triassic to Jurassic

One of the earliest dinosaurs, Saltopus *weighed no more than a house cat.*

Plesiosaur

Ancient Sea Serpents

While the dinosaurs were developing on land, other reptiles returned to the seas, having adapted to life there. Among these were the plesiosaurs (PLEEZ-ee-o-sorz), or "near lizards." The legs of these reptiles developed into fins, and they used their tails to propel themselves through the water.

Kronosaurus (kro-no-SOR-us), a short-necked plesiosaur, was 42 feet long and had huge, eight-foot-long jaws lined with stabbing teeth. *Kronosaurus* probably used its powerful jaws to devour other marine reptiles.

Elasmosaurus (ee-laz-mo-SOR-us) was a long-necked plesiosaur. It was 46 feet long, and half of that was its serpentlike neck. An excellent swimmer, it could move not only forward through the water, but backward, too. This ancient "sea serpent" could not dive well, though, so it cruised near the water's surface with its long neck arched high in the air. When a fish swam close by, *Elasmosaurus* struck like a snake, grasping its wriggling prey with needle-sharp teeth. Although normally a water dweller, this reptile may have laid its eggs on land, using its strong flippers to drag itself ashore.

Some people claim that a plesiosaur named "Nessie" still lives in the dark waters of Scotland's Loch Ness. This 900-foot-deep lake lies along a fault in the earth's crust. Some say that millions of years ago the fault slipped and cut off an arm of the sea, trapping one or several plesiosaurs. Even if that were true, it's doubtful that such creatures endured to the present day. Only 10,000 years ago, an ice age gripped Scotland. At that time the waters of Loch Ness probably froze, making it unlikely that a creature such as the plesiosaur could survive.

Jurassic to Cretaceous

Strange sea serpents like Elasmosaurus *dominated the prehistoric oceans.*

Reptiles in the Air

Dragonflies with three-foot-wide wingspans buzzed in the Mesozoic skies, but they were not alone up there. As early as the Triassic Period, reptiles called pterosaurs (TAIR-o-sorz) had taken to the air. They flew on leathery wings of skin supported by a very long fourth finger. Pterosaurs are so strange that each discovery of a new pterosaur fossil provides more questions than answers. For example: Did they fly or glide through the air? Did they take off from the ground or launch themselves from cliffs? Complicating matters is the fact that there were not just two or three kinds of pterosaurs but more than 80 kinds. The answers to the questions may be different for each type.

Pterosaurs did belong to two main groups. Rhamphorhynchoids (ram-fo-RINK-oydz), the first to develop, lived during the Triassic Period. They were robin- to hawk-sized, with short jaws and necks and long tails with a small blade of bone at the end. Soviet scientists discovered the remains of such a creature that in life appears to have been covered by two-inch-long fur. They named it *Sordes pilosus* (SOR-deez pil-O-sus), or "hairy devil."

The pterodactyloids (tair-uh-DAK-til-oydz) developed in the Jurassic and Cretaceous periods. They had long necks and wings, but just a stub of a tail. The first were pigeon-sized, but that soon changed. *Pteranodon* (tair-AN-o-don), or "winged and toothless," was about the size of a turkey, but it had a wingspan nearly as wide as a school bus is long. An even greater giant, named *Quetzalcoatlus* (ket-zal-kuh-WAHT-lus), had a wingspan of about 35 feet, or that of a small aircraft!
Triassic to Cretaceous

More than 80 kinds of pterosaurs, like this hairy Sordes pilosus, *filled the prehistoric skies.*

The Giants

Can you imagine a creature weighing more than 60,000 pounds, or as much as 95 cubic feet of solid lead? *Apatosaurus* ("deceptive lizard") did and it wasn't even the largest of the Jurassic giants known as the sauropods ("lizard feet"). *Supersaurus* weighed some 160,000 pounds, and *Ultrasaurus* may have weighed even more. *Apatosaurus* stood 15 feet high at the shoulder, but *Brachiosaurus* ("arm lizard") may have topped 20 feet. *Apatosaurus* was 70 feet long from nose to tail, but *Seismosaurus* may have been 120 feet long, long enough to span nearly the width of a football field. These incredible animals were the largest to ever walk the earth.

Can you think of any reasons why large size would have been an advantage to a dinosaur? For one, it made it easier to stay warm. The larger a creature is, the more slowly it gives off heat. (Likewise, a small cup of broth will cool much faster than a large pot of it.) Large size is also a good defense. When attacked, a huge sauropod probably reared up and crushed an enemy beneath its strong, pillar-like legs, or it used its heavy tail to knock an attacker such as *Allosaurus* ("strange lizard") off its feet.

Large size did present some problems, however. These giants had to eat from 500 to 1,000 pounds of leaves every day. Finding that much food all the time may not have been easy. They certainly could eat fast, though, because they didn't chew their food but swallowed it in gulps. To help digest such meals, a sauropod swallowed rough stones called gastroliths ("stomach stones"). When the dinosaur's stomach muscles moved, the stones would grind the food!
Jurassic

Giant Brachiosaurus *defended itself from* Ceratosaurus, *a ferocious meat-eater of the Jurassic Period.*

Plates and Spikes

When you look at a picture of a *Stegosaurus* ("roofed lizard"), the first thing you notice is an unusual row (or "roof") of triangular-shaped plates along its back. Scientists are not certain how *Stegosaurus* used these bony plates, or whether the strange plates were arranged in one row or two. One suggestion is that the plates, the largest of which were three feet high and three feet wide, helped the dinosaur to control its body temperature. There were numerous fine grooves on both sides of each plate. Perhaps a web of blood vessels was located in these grooves just beneath the skin, and *Stegosaurus* exposed the plates to sunlight in order to warm its blood. Perhaps when the creature needed to cool its blood down, it turned its body and plates away from the direct rays of the sun.

At 30 feet long and between two and three tons in weight, *Stegosaurus* was a large dinosaur. Still, it may have had to protect itself from ferocious Jurassic predators. Bony knobs on its throat probably gave it some protection from slashing teeth and claws, but *Stegosaurus*'s best weapons lay at the end of its heavy tail: four sharp spikes, each about three feet long, which the dinosaur could thrash about.

Although much smaller than *Stegosaurus*, *Kentrosaurus*, or "spiked lizard," had an even greater arsenal of armory. Small plates crowning its neck and shoulders led to a double row of sharp spikes along its back and tail. Long spikes also jutted out from each hip. The predators of the plant-eating *Kentrosaurus* must have thought twice before attacking their heavily armored prey!

Jurassic

Protected by sharp spikes and plates, plant-eating Kentrosaurus *tromped through the foliage.*

The Boneheads

Over the millions of years they lived on the earth, the dinosaurs developed an amazing array of claws, spikes, plates, armor, crests, and horns. One of the oddest such features was the dinosaur "crash helmet." One animal with this strange trait was *Stegoceras* (steg-o-SAIR-us). This seven-foot-long creature's dome-shaped skull was several inches thick. The skull was also trimmed with a wreath of knobby bone, earning the dinosaur the name "horned roof." *Stegoceras*'s huge relative *Pachycephalosaurus* (pak-ee-cef-uh-lo-SOR-us), or "thick-headed lizard," also deserved its name. This 15-foot-long plant-eater's skull was topped by a bony dome 10 inches thick—20 times thicker than a human skull!

Surprisingly, scientists believe that *Pachycephalosaurus* did not use its special headgear as a weapon to fight enemies, but rather to battle other members of its own species in tests of strength. It's likely that *Pachycephalosaurus* was a mountain dweller that lived in small herds or flocks. When a male wished to win a mate or challenge the leader of the herd, he probably had to engage in a "butting contest" with another male. As rams do today, these dinosaurs charged at each other headfirst, crashing together with a loud crack. Having a thick, strong skull was thus definitely an advantage. The bones of the males' back and tail were also strong enough to take the terrible battering, and they were probably well padded with shock-absorbing cartilage. Most likely these creatures didn't fight to the death, but after a few collisions, one of the rivals gave up and let the winner claim his prize.

Cretaceous

Pachycephalosauruses *challenged one another to a "butting contest" for domination of the terrain.*

The Armored Tanks

If you crossed a gigantic turtle with an armored tank, you might get a creature like *Ankylosaurus* (an-KY-lo-SOR-us). This dinosaur was 30 feet long and 15 feet wide. *Ankylosaurus,* or "stiff lizard," could repel just about any sort of attack. Protective bony plates, spikes, and studs covered its back and sides, and hornlike spikes stood out from its thick, strong skull. Even its eyes were protected by bony lids. This dinosaur was also equipped with strong, curved claws on its feet. When attacked it probably used these claws to dig into the ground and hold on tight.

Ankylosaurus's armor did not cover its entire body, however. Its one unprotected part was its belly. All an attacker, such as *Tyrannosaurus rex,* had to do was simply turn the armored dinosaur over on its back. Of course, this was probably a lot more trouble than it was worth, because if *Ankylosaurus* preferred to fight, it had the perfect weapon: a large, bony knob at the end of its long tail. By swinging its tail like a club, *Ankylosaurus* may have been able to knock an enemy off its feet or even break its leg. A meat-eater with a broken leg would not be able to attack again and would soon die of starvation.

Many kinds of ankylosaurs were common at the end of the Cretaceous Period. Their remains have been found even in the Antarctic. A nest of six German shepherd–sized baby ankylosaurs was found in the Gobi Desert in 1988. Five were discovered huddled close together and another was, in one scientist's words, "curled up like a sleeping dog."
Cretaceous

Ankylosaurs, built like armored tanks, fought attackers—and each other—with their clublike tails.

Chasmosaurus skull

Horns and Frills

The bird-hipped dinosaurs, or ornithicians, were divided into three main groups. Ankylosaurs (which you just read about) and duckbilled dinosaurs (which you will meet later in this book) were two. Some of the best-known dinosaurs belonged to the third group: the ceratopsians (sair-uh-TOP-see-unz), or "horned face" dinosaurs. The largest ceratopsian was the incredible 27,000-pound, 30-foot-long *Triceratops* (try-SAIR-uh-tops). *Triceratops* means "three-horned face," and you can easily see why scientists gave this creature that name. A thick, stubby horn extended from its snout, and above its eyes were two bony horns that sometimes grew to four feet long.

Triceratops, a plant-eater, had a strong beak for clipping branches and twigs. It also had a short neck frill (a flattened extension of the skull that could cover the neck like a shield) made of a sheet of solid bone. Although *Triceratops* didn't look for trouble, it was certainly able to handle it. This dinosaur was as sturdy as a tank and as tall as an elephant, and it may have been able to run up to 30 miles per hour. A herd of angry *Triceratops* with their horns lowered could probably persuade a hungry meat-eater to hunt elsewhere.

Another impressive ceratopsian was *Chasmosaurus* (kaz-mo-SOR-us), or "cleft lizard." It had a most unusual frill that was even longer than the animal's skull. Such a frill would have been too heavy for the animal to hold up were it not for the large, skin-covered openings in the bone that probably lightened it. Scientists believe that the bony frill served to anchor jaw muscles that powered *Chasmosaurus*'s strong bite. It also made an effective display, to discourage predators and to attract a mate.

Cretaceous

Plant-eating Triceratops *frightened away possible attackers with its three fierce horns.*

The Tyrant King

Tyrannosaurus rex ("king tyrant lizard") was well suited to its role as the earth's most terrifying flesh-eater of all time. Its three-foot-long jaws were packed with sharp teeth that grew up to seven inches long. This fierce dinosaur's powerful neck muscles allowed it to snap and slash continuously at its prey. If that doesn't sound frightening enough, imagine such ferocity in a creature that was 45 feet long, tall enough to peer into a second-story window, and that weighed in at about 16,000 pounds.

Some scientists think that *Tyrannosaurus rex* was too big and slow to have been a predator and that it was a scavenger, an animal that eats the bodies of dead animals. Although this is possible, the creature was probably a good hunter, too. In fact, there is some evidence that *Tyrannosaurus* had stereoscopic vision (and it may have been the only large meat-eater to have such vision). That means it could focus both eyes on a victim at once, which made it possible to judge the creature's distance. Also, *Tyrannosaurus*'s neck and head were heavily reinforced, probably to withstand the blows from a struggling victim.

Unbelievably, this gigantic creature had tiny, nearly useless arms that were no longer than those of an adult human. Although its fingers were tipped with sharp claws, *Tyrannosaurus*'s hands were too short to have been used as weapons. In fact, at less than three feet long, the arms were too short to reach the dinosaur's mouth and so were useless for feeding as well. The purpose, if any, of *Tyrannosaurus*'s tiny arms is a mystery that scientists are still trying to solve. What do you think?

Cretaceous

Fierce Tyrannosaurus rex *probably hunted any creature in sight to satisfy its carnivorous appetite.*

(male) *Parasaurolophus*   *Corythosaurus*   *Lambeosaurus*   *Saurolophus*

The Duckbills

Have you ever thought about what dinosaurs may have sounded like? The third group of ornithicians, known as the duckbills, or hadrosaurs (HAD-ro-sorz), may have roared, tooted, snorted, and whistled! Many duckbills sported hollow bony crests on their heads that held air passages. These crests were perfect for amplifying, or boosting, sound when the animal breathed.

Corythosaurus (ko-rith-o-SOR-us), or "helmet lizard," had a crest like half a dinner plate. The tubelike crest of *Parasaurolophus* (pair-uh-sor-uh-LOF-us), or "almost a ridged lizard," arched backward more than four feet. These crests probably served several purposes. Perhaps their shape or color helped the animals to recognize each other. The sounds they made could have been useful for recognition as well, or to give a warning when danger was near. Males may have trumpeted loudly through their impressive crests when competing for a mate. In some duckbills, the arrangement of the air passages through the crest may have even enhanced their sense of smell.

Not all the duckbill dinosaurs had crests, but they were similar in other ways. For example, they usually walked upright, and, not surprisingly, they all had flattened snouts like a duck's beak. The beak ended in a down-turned cutting edge for snipping off tough leaves and twigs. The animals chewed their food with an arsenal of up to 1,000 teeth. That's an amazing number of teeth when you realize that adult humans get by with only 32 teeth.

Duckbills of a given kind lived in large groups for protection. As the seasons changed from wet to dry, these dinosaurs migrated in huge herds searching for food. Can you imagine how an area would be changed if thousands of plant-eating creatures, each weighing two or three tons, trampled through?

Cretaceous

The female Parasaurolophus's *crest was smaller than the male's. Crests of other duckbills varied as well.*

Dangerous Deinonychus

Deinonychus (dy-no-NYK-us) was not a large dinosaur. It was about 8 to 10 feet long from nose to tail and weighed only 100 to 200 pounds. Still, it may have been among the most dangerous creatures of the Cretaceous Period.

Remains of this animal were first discovered in 1964 by John Ostrom. It was easy to see that this dinosaur must have been very agile. Its slender tail, stiffened by bony rods, could be held up high to help *Deinonychus* keep its balance, and it had long, slim hind legs. But this dinosaur's feet caught scientists by surprise—one toe on each foot was tipped with a savage, curved claw about five inches long. By balancing on one hind foot, *Deinonychus*, or "terrible claw," could slash and tear at a victim with this deadly weapon. When not in use, the huge claw was held up off the ground to keep it safe from wear. The creature also had long-fingered hands tipped with short but sharp claws. These hands could be held palm to palm to grasp and hold struggling prey.

Although *Deinonychus* was most likely a cunning hunter, it probably didn't work alone. Some scientists think these fierce dinosaurs roamed in packs, just as modern wolves do. By cooperating, they would have been able to bring down very large animals many times their own size, such as the 20-foot-long *Tenontosaurus* (tuh-NON-toe-sor-us). Bones of this 2,000-pound plant-eater have been discovered surrounded by the bones of *Deinonychus*. This suggests a possible predator/prey relationship between these creatures.

Cretaceous

Armed with their single enormous claws, Deinonychuses *could attack dinosaurs many times their size.*

Speed Demons

For short distances, the fastest humans can run at a little more than 20 miles per hour. That wouldn't have been fast enough to outrun the family of speedy dinosaurs known as the ornithomimids (or-nith-o-MYM-idz), or "bird mimics." At about 13 feet long, *Gallimimus* ("rooster mimic") was the largest of this family that lived during the Cretaceous Period. Running on its powerful hind legs, it could sprint as fast as 35 miles per hour.

The ornithomimids were so named because, when piecing together the way they looked and moved, their discoverers were reminded of birds. *Struthiomimus* (stroo-thee-o-MYM-us), or "ostrich mimic," looked a lot like the modern bird it is named for. Although smaller than *Gallimimus*, it could run just as quickly.

Are you wondering how scientists can tell how fast a dinosaur could run? If they know how large a dinosaur was, scientists can figure out how fast it ran by measuring its stride in fossil footprints. (Stride is the distance between two footprints made by the same foot.) The faster an animal runs, the farther apart the prints will be. The distance between prints also depends on the creature's size. In one step a very large, *slow-moving* animal can cover the same distance as a *running* small animal.

There are two reasons why speed would have been valuable to the ornithomimids. Besides fruit and seeds, the bird mimics ate lizards and insects. They would have to be fast to snare such swift prey. The second reason was that being lightly built, with only slender, toothless beaks, these dinosaurs had very little with which to protect themselves from hungry meat-eaters. The speedy ornithomimids most likely found it a safer practice to run from danger than to challenge a ferocious predator.

Cretaceous

Gallimimus's best self-defense against a hungry carnivore was its speed.

The Fishing Dinosaur

How would you like to have a dinosaur named after you? Amateur fossil collector Bill Walker has that honor. One cold January day in 1983, while searching for fossils in a quarry near London, he noticed something odd sticking out from the clay. On closer inspection, it turned out to be an enormous claw nearly 15 inches long. Walker reported his find and scientists were quick to investigate. When some bones were removed from the quarry, the scientists realized that there were actually two claws and that they belonged on the animal's hands rather than on its feet. They named the dinosaur *Baryonyx walkeri* (bar-ee-ON-iks wal-KAIR-ee), or "Walker's heavy claw."

The strange creature measured 20 feet long and weighed nearly 4,000 pounds. Investigators quickly saw that this was a very different sort of dinosaur. It had a flattened, crocodilelike snout with 128 sharp teeth. That's twice as many as most flesh-eating dinosaurs had. Its long neck was not very flexible and lacked the S-shaped curve of other large predators. *Baryonyx walkeri* differed from most meat-eaters in another way, too: It sported very powerful forelimbs. But what was the purpose of the incredible claws? *Baryonyx*'s sturdy arms and slashing claws may have been a good defense against its enemies. Fish scales found within the animal's body cavity provide another answer: *Baryonyx* was a fishing dinosaur. It lived near rivers or lakeshores. Crouching on a bank, it possibly waited until a fish such as *Lepidotes* swam close, and then, with its hooklike claw, it pierced the prey and pulled it out of the water. *Baryonyx* probably did not survive on a diet of fish alone, however. It may also have been a scavenger.
Cretaceous

Fish-eating Baryonyx walkeri *used its deadly sharp claws to fish for its prey.*

Sail-Backed Dinosaurs

Using solar panels for temperature regulation is not a new idea. A few dinosaurs had tall splendid sails on their backs that may have been used as heat exchangers to warm or cool the animals. *Spinosaurus* (spyn-o-SOR-us), or "spined lizard," was nearly 40 feet long. The long jaws and sharp teeth of this ferocious meat-eater were impressive, but its most noticeable feature was its huge sail. The sail was formed by leathery skin that stretched across a fan of supporting spines. The longest spines were six feet high, or as tall as a human adult male.

When fierce, meat-eating *Spinosaurus* woke after a cool night, it probably lounged for a while with its sail exposed to the warming sun. The sail was filled with blood vessels, and the sun's heat could be quickly absorbed by the blood near the surface. The warmed blood could then be carried to all parts of the creature's body. The burst of energy available through rapid warming gave this deadly predator a tremendous advantage over prey that was still slow and sluggish from the long night. *Spinosaurus* most likely needed a way to cool off as well, since it lived in the dry hot lands of what is now northern Africa. So it simply angled its sail away from the direct rays of the sun, and cooling breezes did the trick.

Meat-eaters weren't the only dinosaurs to develop sails. A plant-eating neighbor of *Spinosaurus* also had one. The sail of *Ouranosaurus* (oo-ran-o-SOR-us), or "brave monitor lizard," was much shorter. However, unlike that of *Spinosaurus*, the sail continued from *Ouranosaurus*'s back all the way to the end of its tail and probably worked just as well.

Cretaceous

The huge sail on the back of Spinosaurus *may have served as a heat-regulating system.*

The Colorful Dinosaurs

For many years, dinosaurs in books have been painted in dull shades of gray, brown, and green. Now scientists say that many of these remarkable reptiles may have been brightly colored and patterned, and they have several good reasons for thinking so.

For example, fossil impressions of dinosaur skin show that it was not smooth but highly textured. In modern reptiles, such texture is often associated with color. In preserved dinosaur skin, the pigment cells, or color cells, didn't survive, but the patterns made by raised scales show up clearly. Plant-eaters often had tiny rosettes of flattened scales. Meat-eaters sported rough clusters of scales raised as much as two inches above the surface. These textured areas may have been colored as well.

Also, modern animals are very colorful, with dazzling patterns and markings used for display or camouflage. There's no reason why the dinosaurs should have been any different. The crests of large duckbills such as *Lambeosaurus* (lam-bee-o-SOR-us), or "Lambe's lizard," may have been brightly colored to attract mates. Perhaps the huge frill of *Chasmosaurus* was decorated to draw attention to its size. Markings that helped them blend into their surroundings would have been a great advantage to many plant-eating dinosaurs. Predators, too, may have benefited from patterns that disguised them as they lurked in ambush for unsuspecting prey. So stripes on *Tyrannosaurus rex*? Why not!

Cretaceous

Colorful Lambeosaurus *drew attention to itself with its brightly patterned skin.*

South America: The Island

By the time of the Cretaceous Period, the great supercontinent Pangaea was just a memory. It had broken up and begun to form smaller continents. The land that would someday be South America was only an island. For millions of years, the animals that lived on this gigantic island were separated from others of their kind. Many of these creatures, particularly the sauropods, changed dramatically. In the rest of the world, the great sauropods such as *Apatosaurus* had become extinct by the early Cretaceous Period. In the competition for food, they had lost to the more efficient duckbill dinosaurs. This was not the case in South America, where plant-eating sauropods thrived until the end of the Mesozoic Era. Their development took a strange turn, though, and the first armored sauropods, such as *Saltasaurus* ("lizard from Salta"), appeared.

Saltasaurus was not as large as its relatives on northern land masses, so size was not its main defense against meat-eaters. This 40-foot-long dinosaur had something else. Its thick skin was studded with thousands of tiny bony spikes. Four-inch plates of ridged bone lined the animal's neck and back. Although *Tyrannosaurus rex* did not roam on the South American island, an almost equally fierce predator did. Called *Carnotaurus,* this unusual beast had powerful jaw and neck muscles, and large bony horns protruded above its eyes. Although *Carnotaurus* was surely quite ferocious, when looking for a meal it probably avoided the well-protected *Saltasaurus.*
Cretaceous

Prehistoric South America—a lush island inhabited by such well-armored giants as Saltasaurus.

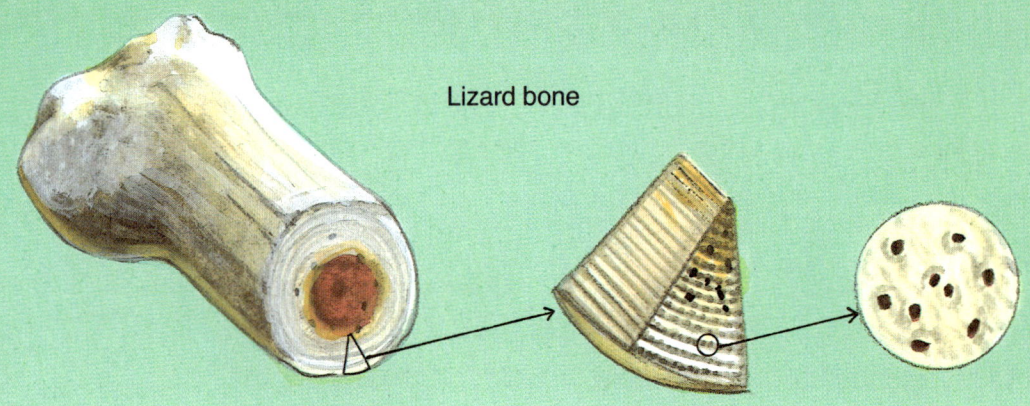
Lizard bone

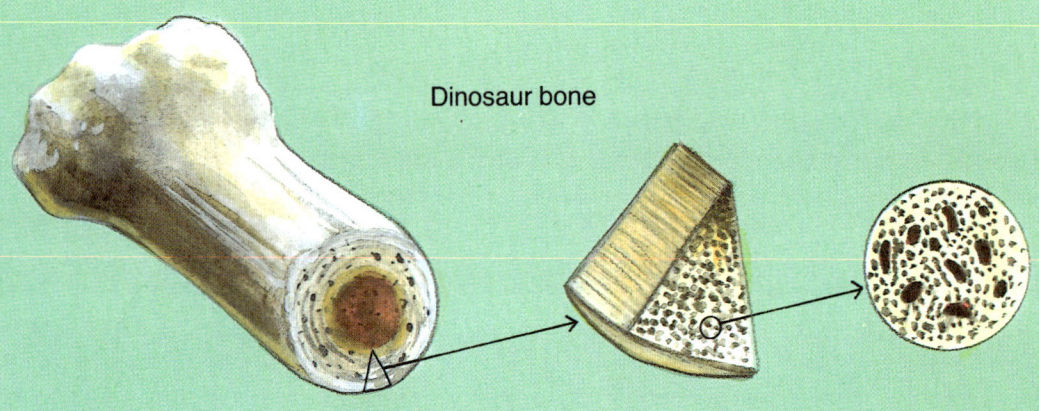
Dinosaur bone

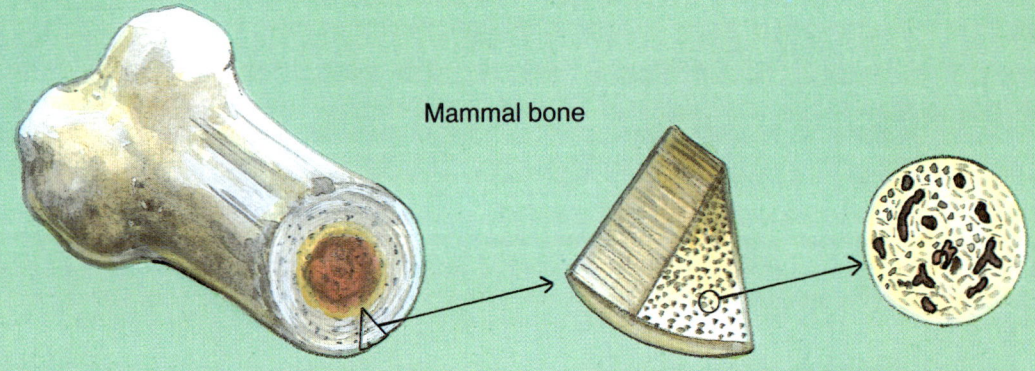
Mammal bone

Warm Blood or Cold Blood?

Scientists who first studied the dinosaurs found them similar to modern reptiles. They were scaly, laid eggs, and had uniformly shaped teeth. The scientists assumed that dinosaurs, like modern reptiles, were cold-blooded. That means that their body temperature was not controlled internally but by the temperature of the environment. Now there is evidence that some dinosaurs may have been warm-blooded.

Whether dinosaurs were warm-blooded would be an easy question to answer if their hearts and lungs had been fossilized along with their bones. (These organs are more complex in warm-blooded animals than in cold-blooded ones.) But these soft parts rotted away before the animals were preserved in stone. Still, some clues survive in the bones. By comparing fossil babies with fossil adults, researchers suspect that the growth rate of certain dinosaurs was faster than that of most reptiles and more like the growth rate of mammals. Also, dinosaur bones are riddled with tiny channels. These channels are found in the bones of warm-blooded creatures, too. Scientists point out, however, that the channels also exist in large cold-blooded crocodiles.

The case for small warm-blooded dinosaurs may be stronger. Generally, these animals were not slow and sluggish like most cold-blooded creatures are. Many were able to run at fairly high speeds. Some small meat-eaters appear to have stalked prey for long distances or engaged in battles that required a great deal of energy. It's even possible that one small dinosaur, *Avimimus* (ahv-ih-MYM-us), or "bird mimic," had a featherlike covering that kept body heat in, as it does in warm-blooded birds. The verdict is not yet in, but the evidence in favor of at least some warm-blooded dinosaurs is mounting.

A close look at dinosaur bone shows that it is riddled with the tiny channels common in mammal bone.

Archaeopteryx: Bird or Dinosaur?

Millions of years ago, during the late Jurassic Period, a very small, reptilelike creature died. Its body came to rest on the bottom of a warm, peaceful lagoon, and there it was slowly covered with mud. Its death probably went completely unnoticed. For 150 million years, it lay undisturbed. But when the little animal's remains were uncovered in a German quarry in 1861, the entire scientific world took notice. The fossil evidence showed that, when it was alive, this creature had been covered with feathers!

But was it a feathered *dinosaur*? No. *Archaeopteryx* (ar-kee-OP-ter-iks) was a bird of sorts, perhaps the first bird. It had a fused collarbone, or wishbone, as all birds do, but it lacked the keeled breastbone that enables birds to fly long distances. This little animal probably took to the air in short leaps and glides. Its hind claws were straighter than those of birds that perch in trees, and it most likely spent much of its time on the ground.

Archaeopteryx also had many characteristics similar to those of small dinosaurs. A little more than a foot long, it resembled *Compsognathus*. It had the tail and teeth of a reptile and small, clawed hands. It's quite likely that *Archaeopteryx,* or "ancient wing," descended from the coelurosaurs (see-LOO-ro-sorz), which were small, meat-eating dinosaurs. It is also possible that modern true birds are also descended from the dinosaurs. In fact, as paleontologist John Ostrom once said, "Dinosaurs didn't become extinct. They simply flew away."
Jurassic

Archaeopteryx, *perhaps the first bird, resembled a reptile with its tail, claws, and sharp teeth.*

The Dinosaur Egg

In the early 1920s, Roy Chapman Andrews set out into the Gobi Desert to search for the bones of our human ancestors. Braving scorching heat, howling dust storms, terrible thirst, and even bandits, Andrews found something entirely different in the rust-colored sand: dinosaur eggs! The eight-inch-long eggs were shaped roughly like long ovals slightly tapered at one end. They rested in a spiral pattern, with the tapered ends facing outward. This suggests that the mother either moved around the nest as she laid her eggs, or positioned them after they were laid. When discovered, the eggs were flattened and slightly crushed, probably by the very rocks and sediment that preserved them. A pony-sized dinosaur known as *Protoceratops* ("first horned face") had dug the bowl-shaped nest. Andrews uncovered the remains of a different dinosaur, too, just above another *Protoceratops* nest. It had a powerful, toothless beak that was well suited for crushing eggs. In fact, this second dinosaur had probably been raiding the nest when it died, and so it was named *Oviraptor*, or "egg stealer."

Since Andrews's incredible finds, many dinosaur eggs have been discovered. The largest belonged to the 40-foot-long *Hypselosaurus* (hip-seh-lo-SOR-us), or "high-ridged lizard." The baby that would have hatched from that football-sized egg would have weighed about two pounds, but it would have grown to weigh 20,000 pounds as an adult! Even the eggs of the largest dinosaurs probably weren't any bigger than those of *Hypselosaurus*. That's because eggshells have to be thick enough to support their own overall size. The shell of a gigantic egg would have been too thick for a weak baby dinosaur to break out of.
Cretaceous

These dinosaur eggs once hatched Protoceratops, *which grew to weigh 20,000 pounds as adults.*

Dinosaur Nurseries

Paleontologist Jack Horner found his first dinosaur bone in Montana when he was seven years old. Less than 30 years later and about 30 miles from the site of his first discovery, he made another. It was a site so filled with dinosaur nests and eggs that he named it "Egg Mountain." Prior to Horner's find, few scientists thought of dinosaurs as good parents. The evidence on Egg Mountain showed that some were. In fact, Horner called one 30-foot-long resident of the site *Maiasaura* (my-uh-SOR-uh), or "good mother lizard."

Maiasaura joined hundreds of others of its kind that laid eggs and raised their young in areas known as nurseries. Amazingly, the *Maiasaura* returned to the same nursery sites year after year. They dug mud nests about 7 feet across and 25 feet apart. After the eggs were laid, they were covered with a blanket of leaves. Scientists have concluded that the small spaces discovered above fossil nests were left behind when the leafy blankets rotted away.

The young dinosaurs were helpless when born and needed the care of their mothers, who brought the youngsters food until they were strong enough to find their own. The babies must have needed a lot of food, for they grew very quickly. A baby *Maiasaura*, for example, was about 13 inches long when it hatched and weighed less than two pounds. However, it grew much faster than a human baby does. Once it reached about four months of age and a length of five feet, it was ready to leave the nest for good. By the time the youngster's first birthday rolled around, this little "baby" could be 10 feet long and weigh 750 pounds!
Cretaceous

Maiasaura *newborns, about two pounds at birth, weighed 750 pounds by their first birthday.*

An Enemy from Space?

Have you wondered why there are no dinosaurs alive today? About 65 MYA something ended their reign. Although there are dozens of theories, no one really knows what happened. A popular idea is that, around that time, a huge comet, possibly six miles wide, slammed into Earth. Scientists theorize that the tremendous impact not only created a huge crater, but also changed conditions on the planet dramatically. The vaporized comet threw thousands of tons of dust into the air. Temperatures at the center of the impact could have been three times hotter than the surface of the sun. Forests burst into flames. The resulting firestorms sent ash and smoke into the atmosphere. Shrouded in a worldwide cloud of dust and smoke that blocked out most sunlight, the earth cooled. Without enough sunlight, a great deal of land and ocean plant life died during this "unnatural winter." Without plants to eat, the plant-eating dinosaurs soon followed. Finally, deprived of prey, the meat-eaters died off as well.

Evidence to support the comet theory exists in a layer of clay that was laid down at the time of extinction. The amount of a metal called iridium contained in this layer is at least 30 times higher than in the layers above and below it. This metal, rare in the earth's crust, is relatively common in comets and asteroids. Also, soot levels in the layer—possible evidence of firestorms—are thousands of times higher than normal. Still, there are other possible explanations for such findings. Volcanoes, too, are an earthly source of iridium and soot. But no matter what the cause, the results are certain: Eventually, the last dinosaur sighed its final breath and with this sigh, they were all gone forever.

A comet crashing into the earth may have caused an "unnatural winter," leading to the death of the dinosaurs.

Protosuchus
("first crocodile")
Late Triassic Period, 3.3 feet long

Deinosuchus
("terrible crocodile")
Late Cretaceous Period, 49 feet long

Crocodylus
(modern crocodile)
10 feet long

The Survivors

The event or series of events that killed the dinosaurs also eliminated more than two-thirds of the plant and animal species on Earth. But why did one-third survive? Once again, there are many theories. Probably those living things that could adapt quickly and easily to the changing surroundings were able to pull through. Unfortunately, adaptability was probably not a strength of the dinosaurs. Dinosaur species living at the end of the Mesozoic Era were highly specialized to live in very particular environments, or niches. Even slight changes in the surroundings, such as a warming or cooling of the climate, could be harmful to them. Other types of animals, such as small mammals, were less specialized than the dinosaurs and could occupy a wider variety of environments. They could also adapt more easily to new conditions. Still other creatures may have entered into a resting state when the environment changed, somewhat like the hibernation of modern bears. They may have just "waited out" the bad times.

The survivors are not necessarily similar. In fact, they include members of many different animal families. Ancient alligators and crocodiles were as familiar a sight in Laurasia as they are in the tropical waters of today. Turtles made it through, as did snakes, lizards, insects, fishes, and birds. Fortunately for us, mammals, too, were among the survivors. They were small, furry creatures that had first appeared near the end of the Triassic Period. For millions of years, mammals had lived in the shadow of the mighty dinosaurs. When the dinosaurs died, those timid little creatures filled the vacant niches. The Age of the Mammals had begun.

Huge Deinosuchus, *which grew up to 49 feet long, was an ancestor of the modern crocodile.*

The First Mammals

Because you are a mammal, there are several things you have in common with other mammals, from baby rabbits to grizzly bears. All mammals are warm-blooded, or endothermic ("inside heat"). This means that their body temperature is internally controlled and stays fairly constant no matter what the temperature of the outside environment. Most mammals have fur or hair somewhere on their bodies that often helps to keep heat in. Females generally give birth to live young, rather than laying eggs, and produce milk to feed the young. Today, mammals are the dominant life-form on Earth and are found in every environment. The 4,000 or so mammalian species include a wide range of creatures, from tiny rodents, to the huge blue whale, to the remarkable human. It hasn't always been that way.

Megazostrodon (meg-uh-ZAHS-tro-don), or "big-girdled tooth," was probably typical of the first mammals. This shrewlike insect-eater developed about 200 million years ago, during the Mesozoic Era. It was very small—about the size of a modern rat. It may or may not have given birth to live babies, but it had the tooth structure of its modern descendants, and most likely other traits as well. *Megazostrodon* and others like it survived by avoiding the mighty dinosaurs. In daylight, these mammals hid in burrows or under rocky ledges. The furry little animals scurried out to hunt during the cool nights, when most dinosaurs were inactive. When something happened to end the reign of reptiles, somehow our distant mammal ancestors were spared. With most of the dangerous predators gone, new niches in mountains, forests, and grasslands became available to the adaptable little creatures. The death blow to the dinosaurs became the knock of opportunity for the mammals.

Megazostrodon, *an early mammal, had to survive daily attacks from such predators as fierce* Coelophysis.

O. C. Marsh with plaster cast of dinosaur bone

The Bone Wars

A hundred years ago, a shepherd in the American West built a small cabin from old bones he found lying about on the ground. Scientists came across the cabin much later and were astonished to discover that its walls included some 500 bones from ancient turtles, crocodiles, and dinosaurs. At about the same time in Utah, at a place later named Dinosaur National Monument, more than 1,000 dinosaur bones were discovered embedded in a 190-foot-long rock wall. The wall was probably a riverbed that had been lifted and turned upward by the movement of the earth's crust millions of years ago.

To paleontologists Edward Drinker Cope and O. C. Marsh, the American West proved to be a treasure trove of dinosaur fossils. In the late 1800s, the two scientists separately hired teams of fossil hunters to search for new finds. This began a famous rivalry known as the "Bone Wars." The brave hunters had to face harsh weather, lack of transportation, and hostile Indians. It wasn't easy, but each scientist wanted to discover more and better fossils than his rival could. The rush to be the first to describe new species caused some confusion. Cope assembled an ancient reptile and mistakenly placed the animal's head at the wrong end. Marsh named the huge creature he discovered in Colorado *Apatosaurus*. Later he gave a similar animal found in Wyoming the name *Brontosaurus*. Many years afterward, scientists realized that the two animals were one and the same.

Nevertheless, the Bone Wars were very productive. Before they began, only nine North American dinosaur species were known. We have Cope and Marsh to thank for raising that number to more than 140.

Over 130 species of dinosaurs were unearthed during a competitive period called the "Bone Wars."

Mummified *Anatosaurus* skin

The Mummies

Like detectives, paleontologists solve the mysteries of the dinosaurs by searching for clues. Fossils are usually the best source of information. As a rule, however, only the hard parts of an animal, such as the bones and teeth, are preserved. Soft body parts, such as the brain, heart, and skin, rot away. Muscles disappear also, leaving behind only the marks of attachment on bones. Scientists are left with a few clues and a lot of questions.

Luckily, there have been exceptions to the rule that soft body parts are not preserved, and in fact several dinosaur mummies have been found. The mummies formed when the dinosaurs' bodies had a chance to dry out before they decayed. One *Anatosaurus* (uh-NAT-o-SOR-us) mummy was found with some skin and tendons present. The place where the duckbill dinosaur died was probably very warm. In the blazing sun, its skin became tough and leathery. The dinosaur dried and shriveled. Over millions of years, the creature became fossilized.

To the scientists who discovered and studied the *Anatosaurus* mummy, it was truly a buried treasure. The preserved skin showed signs of a speckled pattern. There also seems to have been stretchy skin between the toes. Was it a type of webbing to make the animal a better swimmer? Perhaps it was once thick padding that cushioned the creature's feet as it walked.

Another amazing *Anatosaurus* mummy contained the remains of the dinosaur's last meal. Until this discovery, most people thought that this large hadrosaur spent much of its day in the water, eating soft water plants. The discovery of the preserved stomach contents changed their minds. Before it died, this *Anatosaurus* had dined on tough pine needles, pine cones, and twigs.

A mummified Anatosaurus *allowed scientists to piece together what the dinosaur may have looked like.*

Iguanodon footprint | 9-year-old child's footprint

Dinosaur Trackers

Do you remember how Indians learned about the animals they were hunting by studying the tracks they left behind? Tracks reveal a lot about the creature that made them. In 1802, in the eastern United States, the discovery of huge, birdlike footprints in rock caused a sensation. Now we know that a dinosaur left the tracks as it strolled across a muddy plain millions of years ago. Since that find, many such tracks have been discovered.

A series of tracks in Australia was made by 130 large dinosaurs running at about five miles per hour. For a human, that's a fast trot. Another set of footprints close by hint as to why these animals were in a hurry: They were being followed by a meat-eater. Besides revealing such information about predator/prey relationships, dinosaur footprints also provide important clues about migration patterns. For instance, when researchers found the remains of horned dinosaurs as far apart as southern Canada and within the Arctic Circle, 2,000 miles away, they wondered whether the dinosaurs could have been migrators. The answer was found in the tracks. By measuring stride, scientists figured out how far and fast the animals moved with each step. If the herds kept a steady pace and traveled most of the day, they could have made the trip in about two months.

We also learn from what we *don't* see in the tracks. No tail marks have ever been found, so we know dinosaurs didn't drag their tails on the ground. One set of prints stumped scientists for a while. They were made by a large dinosaur that touched the ground only with its front toes. No, it wasn't dancing. Using its toes to push off along the bottom, the animal was swimming!

Dinosaur tracks left behind millions of years ago have provided scientists with a great deal of information.

Lessons from the Past

The dinosaurs are as interesting as any life-form that has developed since their time. But why do we study animals that have been extinct for 65 million years? For one thing, we can discover much about how life on Earth has changed. Dinosaurs survived successfully for about 160 million years. That's a great deal longer than humans have claimed this planet for their own. By studying dinosaurs, from the small scurrying creatures of the Triassic Period to the skillful hunters of the Cretaceous Period, we learn something about how evolution works. In many instances, dinosaur development appeared to be heading toward larger brain size and sharper senses. In some plant-eating dinosaurs, parental care for the young was becoming more important. Had they survived, the dinosaurs may have developed a high level of intelligence.

In studying dinosaur fossils, we also learn a great deal about the composition and shape of the rock layers that held the fossils for millions of years. The rock layers hold clues to what the ancient earth was like. Evidence of movement of the continents, the rise and fall of mountains, the raising and lowering of sea levels, and major changes in the climate and atmosphere are all recorded in the stone. By learning about these cycles of our planet, we are better able to prepare humankind for the future. So, even though the dinosaurs have been gone for hundreds of centuries, we human inheritors of Planet Earth can still learn valuable lessons from these once mighty creatures.

For Further Reading

Benton, Michael: *Dinosaurs: An A–Z Guide,* New York City, Derrydale Books, 1988.

Dixon, Dougal: *Illustrated Dinosaur Dictionary,* New York City, Gallery Books, 1988.

Elting, Mary, and Goodman, Ann: *Dinosaur Mysteries,* New York City, Platt & Munk, 1980.

Freedman, Russell: *Dinosaurs and Their Young,* New York City, Holiday House, 1983.

Lauber, Patricia: *Dinosaurs Walked Here,* New York City, Bradbury Press, 1987.

Sattler, Helen: *Pterosaurs, the Flying Reptiles,* New York City, Lothrop, Lee & Shepard Books, 1985.

Simon, Seymour: *The Largest Dinosaurs,* New York City, Macmillan Publishing Co., 1986.

Zallinger, Peter: *Dinosaurs and Other Archosaurs,* New York City, Random House, 1986.

Index

Allosaurus 7, 17
Anatosaurus 59
Andrews, Roy Chapman 47
Ankylosaurus 23, 25
Apatosaurus 7, 17, 41, 57
Archaeopteryx 45
Avimimus 43

Baryonyx walkeri 35
birds 45, 53
body temperature
    mammals 55
    reptiles 43
    Spinosaurus 37
    Stegosaurus 19
Brachiosaurus 17

Carnotaurus 41
ceratopsians 25
Chasmosaurus 25, 39
Coelophysis 9, 55
Compsognathus 11, 45
Cope, Edward Drinker 57
Corythosaurus 29
Cretaceous Period 7, 23, 31, 33, 41, 63
crocodiles 43, 53, 57

Deinonychus 31
diet
    Anatosaurus 59
    Baryonyx walkeri 35
    Compsognathus 11
    Deinonychus 31
    hadrosaurs 29
    ornithomimids 33
    Saltopus 11
    sauropods 17
    Triceratops 25
    Tyrannosaurus rex 27
Dinosaur National Monument 57

eggs
    Egg Mountain 49
    Hypselosaurus 47
    Maiasaura 49
    Protoceratops 47
Elasmosaurus 13
Euparkeria 9
extinction 51

fish 35, 53
fossils 43, 63
    Anatosaurus 59
    Antarctic 23
    Archaeopteryx 45
    Baryonyx walkeri 35
    Bone Wars 57
    Deinonychus 31
    dinosaur skin 39
    eggs 47, 49
    footprints 33
    Gobi Desert 23
    pterosaurs 15
    tracks 61

Gallimimus 33
gastroliths 17
Gobi Desert 23, 47
Gondwanaland 7

hadrosaurs 29, 59
Horner, Jack 49
Hypselosaurus 47

insects 11, 53
    dragonflies 15

Jurassic Period 7, 11, 15, 17, 19, 45

Kentrosaurus 19
Kronosaurus 13

Lambeosaurus 39
Laurasia 7, 53
Lepidotes 35
lizards 11, 53
Loch Ness 13

Maiasaura 49
mammals 43, 53, 55
marine reptiles 13
Marsh, O. C. 57
Megazostrodon 55
Mesozoic Era 7, 9, 41, 53, 55

ornithicians 11, 25, 29
ornithomimids 33
Ostrom, John 31, 45
Ouranosaurus 37
Oviraptor 47
Owen, Richard 5

Pachycephalosaurus 21
Pangaea 7, 41
Parasaurolophus 29
Permian Period 9
plants
    cycads 7
    ferns 7
plesiosaurs 13
Protoceratops 47
Pteranodon 15

Quetzalcoatlus 15

rhamphorhynchoids 15

Saltasaurus 41
Saltopus 11
sauricians 11
sauropods 17, 41
Seismosaurus 17
snakes 53
Sordes pilosus 15
South America 41
speed
    body temperature 43
    ornithomimids 33
    stride 33, 61
    Triceratops 25
Spinosaurus 37
Stegoceras 21
Stegosaurus 19
stride 33, 61
Struthiomimus 33
Supersaurus 17

teeth
    Archaeopteryx 45
    Baryonyx walkeri 35
    Elasmosaurus 13
    hadrosaurs 29
    Kronosaurus 13
    reptiles 43
    thecodont 9
    Tyrannosaurus rex 27
Tenontosaurus 31
thecodonts 9
Triassic Period 7, 9, 11, 15, 53, 63
Triceratops 25
turtles 53, 57
Tyrannosaurus rex 7, 23, 27, 39, 41

Ultrasaurus 17